My Healthy Habits

SAFETY FIRST

Norwood House Press

Madison Parker

Cataloging-in-Publication Data

Names: Parker, Madison.
Title: Safety first / Madison Parker.
Description: Buffalo, NY : Norwood House Press, 2026. | Series: My healthy habits | Includes glossary and index.
Identifiers: ISBN 9781978575400 (pbk.) | ISBN 9781978575417 (library bound) | ISBN 9781978575424 (ebook)
Subjects: LCSH: Safety education--Juvenile literature.
Classification: LCC HV675.5 P375 2026 | DDC 613.6--dc23

Published in 2026 by
Norwood House Press
2544 Clinton Street
Buffalo, NY 14224

Designer: Rhea Magaro
Editor: Kim Thompson

Photo credits: Cover, p. 1 Sergey Novikov/Shutterstock.com; p. 5 oes/Shutterstock.com; p. 6 PaniYani/Shutterstock.com; p. 7 Evgeny Atamanenko/Shutterstock.com; p. 8 New Africa/Shutterstock.com; p. 9 Inside Creative House/Shutterstock.com; p. 10 Tatevosian Yana/Shutterstock.com; p. 11 atsurkan/Shutterstock.com; p. 12 Tawnya92/Shutterstock.com; p. 13 Mergeldea/Shutterstock.com; p. 15 Mirror Images/Shutterstock.com; pp. 16, 17 Lukas Jonaitis/Shutterstock.com; p. 18 AlikeYou/Shutterstock.com; p. 19 Krasula/Shutterstock.com; p. 21 kornnphoto/Shutterstock.com;

Printed in the United States of America

CPSIA compliance information: Batch #CSNHP26: For further information contact Norwood House Press at 1-800-237-9932.

TABLE OF CONTENTS

SAFETY IS IMPORTANT

Thinking about safety is important for protecting yourself and the people around you. Staying safe keeps you healthy and happy. By practicing simple safety **habits**, you can feel **confident** and ready for anything!

STREET SAFETY

When you cross the street, always stop and look both ways for cars. It is safest to cross at **crosswalks** after you wait for the walk **signal**.

When riding a bike, wear your helmet and follow the rules. Remember to ride on the right side of the road or path and use hand signals.

You should always wear your seatbelt when you ride in a car.

Stay seated on the school bus. When you get off the bus, walk in front of the bus so the driver can see you.

SUN SAFETY

Sunscreen helps protect your skin from the sun's harmful rays. Wearing a hat and sunglasses keeps your face and eyes safe from strong sunlight.

Staying in the shade when the sun is strongest helps keep you cool. Drinking water keeps you from getting **overheated**.

WATER SAFETY

Always swim close to an adult who can watch you. Wearing a **life preserver** in deep water helps keep you safe. If you are a new swimmer, stay in shallow water.

Follow the pool rules. Walk to **avoid** slipping on the edge of the pool. Never dive unless you know the water is deep enough.

In the ocean or a lake, waves and **currents** can be strong. Boats can zoom by. Stay in **designated** swimming areas near lifeguards.

MAX
DONT SET UP BEHIND US!!!

THUNDERSTORM SAFETY

Go inside if you hear thunder. If you are stuck outside, avoid open spaces, tall trees, and metal objects.

Once you are inside, stay away from windows. Wait until the storm has passed to take a shower or bath.

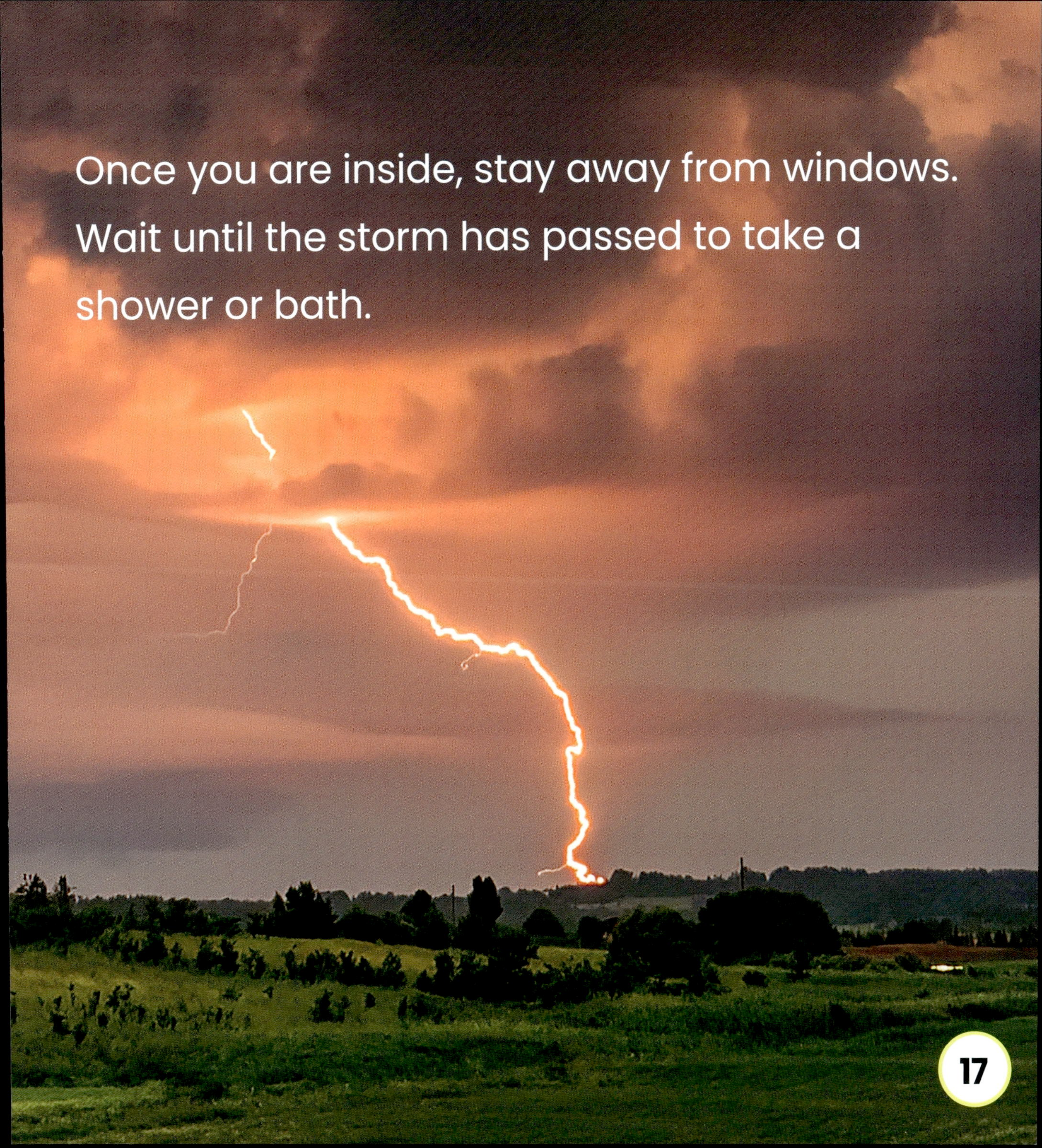

PET SAFETY

Before you pet an animal, always ask its owner. Move slowly and let the pet sniff you first so it feels comfortable.

Be gentle when you play with pets. Avoid pulling on their ears or tails. Give pets their space when they eat and sleep to prevent them from getting scared or upset.

SAFE AND HEALTHY

Thinking about safety every day helps you build healthy habits. Simple actions like wearing a helmet or looking both ways will keep you safe while you are having fun!

GLOSSARY

avoid (uh-VOID): to stay away from something

confident (KAHN-fi-duhnt): a strong belief in your abilities; certain that things will happen in the way you expect

crosswalks (KRAWS-wawks): safe places marked on the street where people can cross

currents (KUR-uhnts): strong movements of water in an ocean or lake that can push you around

designated (DEZ-ig-nay-tid): set aside or marked as a safe place to do something

habits (HAB-itz): activities that you do on a regular basis

life preserver (life pri-ZUR-ver): a vest that makes you float in water so that you do not drown

overheated (oh-vur-HEE-tid): getting too hot, which can make you feel tired or sick

signal (SIG-nuhl): a sign that sends a message or a warning

sunscreen (SUHN-skreen): a lotion or spray that protects your skin from the sun

THINKING QUESTIONS

1. Why is it important to follow safety rules when crossing the street?
2. How does wearing a helmet and using hand signals keep you safe on a bike?
3. What are some ways to protect yourself from the sun?
4. Why should you always swim near an adult or lifeguard?
5. How can you safely approach and play with pets?

INDEX

ABOUT THE AUTHOR

Madison Parker spent her childhood in the city of Chicago, Illinois. A farm girl at heart, today she lives in Wisconsin with her husband and four children on a small farm with cows, goats, chickens, and two miniature horses named Harley and David. Her favorite dessert is vanilla frozen custard with rainbow sprinkles, even in the winter.